Just The
facts101
Textbook Key Facts

Textbook Outlines, Highlights, and Practice Quizzes

Saunders 2014-2015 Strategies for Test Success: Passing Nursing School and the NCLEX Exam

by Linda Anne Silvestri, 1st Edition

All "Just the Facts101" Material Written or Prepared by Cram101 Textbook Reviews

Title Page

OCT 2 4 2014

LEARNING SYSTEM

"Just the Facts101" is a Content Technologies publication and tool designed to give you all the facts from your textbooks. Visit JustTheFacts101.com for the full practice test for each of your chapters for virtually any of your textbooks.

Facts101 has built custom study tools specific to your textbook. We provide all of the factual testable information and unlike traditional study guides, we will never send you back to your textbook for more information.

YOU WILL NEVER HAVE TO HIGHLIGHT A BOOK AGAIN!

Facts101 StudyGuides

All of the information in this StudyGuide is written specifically for your textbook. We include the key terms, places, people, and concepts... the information you can expect on your next exam!

Want to take a practice test?

Throughout each chapter of this StudyGuide you will find links to JustTheFacts101.com where you can select specific chapters to take a complete test on, or you can subscribe and get practice tests for up to 12 of your textbooks, along with other exclusive Jtf101.com tools like problem solving labs and reference libraries.

JustTheFacts101.com

Only Jtf101.com gives you the outlines, highlights, and PRACTICE TESTS specific to your textbook. JustTheFacts101.com is an online application where you'll discover study tools designed to make the most of your limited study time.

By purchasing this book, you get 50% off the normal monthly subscription fee!. Just enter the promotional code **'DK73DW24260'** on the Jtf101.com registration screen.

www.JustTheFacts101.com

ISBN(s): 9781490291673. PUBX-7.201428

Saunders 2014-2015 Strategies for Test Success: Passing Nursing School and the NCLEX Exam
Linda Anne Silvestri, 1st

CONTENTS

1. Preparing for Nursing Examinations 5
2. Developing Study Skills 10
3. Reducing Test Anxiety 17
4. NCLEXe Preparation 22
5. Alternate Item Formats 27
6. How to Avoid Reading into the Question 31
7. Positive and Negative Event Queries 36
8. Questions Requiring Prioritization 39
9. Leading and Managing, Delegating, and Assignment-Making Questions 44
10. Communication Questions 49
11. Pharmacology, Medication, and Intravenous Calculation Questions 53
12. Additional Pyramid Strategies 64
13. Fundamental Skills Questions and Adult Health Questions 69

1. Preparing for Nursing Examinations

CHAPTER OUTLINE: KEY TERMS, PEOPLE, PLACES, CONCEPTS

_____	Semi-vegetarian _____
_____	NCLEX _____
_____	Nursing school _____
_____	Pharmacology _____
_____	Memorization _____
_____	Phenothiazine _____
_____	Syllabus _____

CHAPTER HIGHLIGHTS & NOTES: KEY TERMS, PEOPLE, PLACES, CONCEPTS

Semi-vegetarian	A semi-vegetarian or flexitarian diet is one that is plant-based with the occasional inclusion of meat products. In 2003, the American Dialect Society voted flexitarian as the year's most useful word and defined it as 'a vegetarian who occasionally eats meat'. In 2012, the term was listed for the first time in the mainstream Merriam-Webster's Collegiate Dictionary.
NCLEX	NCLEX is an examination for the licensing of nurses in the United States. There are two types, the NCLEX-RN and the NCLEX-PN.
	NCLEX examinations are developed and owned by the National Council of State Boards of Nursing, Inc. (NCSBN).
Nursing school	A nursing school is a type of educational institution, or part thereof, providing education and training to become a fully qualified nurse. The nature of nursing education and nursing qualifications varies considerably across the world.
Pharmacology	Pharmacology is the branch of medicine and biology concerned with the study of drug action, where a drug can be broadly defined as any man-made, natural, or endogenous (within the cell) molecule which exerts a biochemical and/or physiological effect on the cell, tissue, organ, or organism. More specifically, it is the study of the interactions that occur between a living organism and chemicals that affect normal or abnormal biochemical function.

1. Preparing for Nursing Examinations

Memorization	Memorization is the process of committing something to memory. The act of memorization is often a deliberate mental process undertaken in order to store in memory for later recall items such as experiences, names, appointments, addresses, telephone numbers, lists, stories, poems, pictures, maps, diagrams, facts, music or other visual, auditory, or tactical information. Memorization may also refer to the process of storing particular data into the memory of a device.
Phenothiazine	Phenothiazine is an organic compound that occurs in various antipsychotic and antihistaminic drugs. It has the formula $S(C_6H_4)_2NH$. This yellow tricyclic compound is soluble in acetic acid, benzene, and ether. The compound is related to the thiazine-class of heterocyclic compounds. The phenothiazine structure occurs in various neuroleptic drugs, e.g. chlorpromazine, and antihistaminic drugs, e.g. promethazine. The term 'phenothiazines' describes the largest of the five main classes of neuroleptic antipsychotic drugs. These drugs have antipsychotic and, often, antiemetic properties, although they may also cause severe side effects such as extrapyramidal symptoms (including akathisia and tardive dyskinesia), hyperprolactinaemia, and the rare but potentially fatal neuroleptic malignant syndrome as well as substantial weight gain.
Syllabus	A syllabus, is an outline and summary of topics to be covered in an education or training course. It is descriptive (unlike the prescriptive or specific curriculum). A syllabus is often either set out by an exam board, or prepared by the professor who supervises or controls the course quality.

1. A _____, is an outline and summary of topics to be covered in an education or training course. It is descriptive (unlike the prescriptive or specific curriculum). A _____ is often either set out by an exam board, or prepared by the professor who supervises or controls the course quality.

   a. Theory of multiple intelligences
   b. Memory consolidation
   c. Memory implantation
   d. Syllabus

2. . _____ is an organic compound that occurs in various antipsychotic and antihistaminic drugs. It has the formula $S(C_6H_4)_2NH$. This yellow tricyclic compound is soluble in acetic acid, benzene, and ether. The compound is related to the thiazine-class of heterocyclic compounds.

   The _____ structure occurs in various neuroleptic drugs, e.g. chlorpromazine, and antihistaminic drugs, e.g.

promethazine. The term '_____s' describes the largest of the five main classes of neuroleptic antipsychotic drugs. These drugs have antipsychotic and, often, antiemetic properties, although they may also cause severe side effects such as extrapyramidal symptoms (including akathisia and tardive dyskinesia), hyperprolactinaemia, and the rare but potentially fatal neuroleptic malignant syndrome as well as substantial weight gain.

a. Tissue fluid
b. Memory consolidation
c. Phenothiazine
d. Memory rehearsal

3. _____ is the process of committing something to memory. The act of _____ is often a deliberate mental process undertaken in order to store in memory for later recall items such as experiences, names, appointments, addresses, telephone numbers, lists, stories, poems, pictures, maps, diagrams, facts, music or other visual, auditory, or tactical information. _____ may also refer to the process of storing particular data into the memory of a device.

a. Memory conformity
b. Memory consolidation
c. Memory implantation
d. Memorization

4. _____ is an examination for the licensing of nurses in the United States. There are two types, the _____-RN and the _____-PN.

_____ examinations are developed and owned by the National Council of State Boards of Nursing, Inc. (NCSBN).

a. NCLEX
b. Nightingale ward
c. Notes on Nursing
d. Nurse Licensure Compact

5. A _____ or flexitarian diet is one that is plant-based with the occasional inclusion of meat products. In 2003, the American Dialect Society voted flexitarian as the year's most useful word and defined it as 'a vegetarian who occasionally eats meat'. In 2012, the term was listed for the first time in the mainstream Merriam-Webster's Collegiate Dictionary.

a. Semi-vegetarian
b. Tissue fluid
c. Common Intermediate Language
d. Balanced Budget Act

1. d
2. c
3. d
4. a
5. a

You can take the complete Chapter Practice Test

for 1. Preparing for Nursing Examinations
on all key terms, persons, places, and concepts.

Online 99 Cents

http://www.JustTheFacts101.com

Use www.JustTheFacts101.com for all your study needs

including Facts101's online interactive problem solving labs in

chemistry, statistics, mathematics, and more.

2. Developing Study Skills

	Time management
	Scheduling
	NCLEX
	Procrastination
	Adverse effect
	Energy level
	Estrogen
	Self-assessment
	ABC
	Electrolyte
	Nursing school
	Sims' position
	Content
	Monoamine
	Monoamine oxidase
	Oxidase
	Critical thinking

2. Developing Study Skills

Time management	Time management is the act or process of planning and exercising conscious control over the amount of time spent on specific activities, especially to increase efficiency or productivity. Time management may be aided by a range of skills, tools, and techniques used to manage time when accomplishing specific tasks, projects and goals complying with a due date. This set encompasses a wide scope of activities, and these include planning, allocating, setting goals, delegation, analysis of time spent, monitoring, organizing, scheduling, and prioritizing.
Scheduling	Scheduling is an important tool for manufacturing and engineering, where it can have a major impact on the productivity of a process. In manufacturing, the purpose of scheduling is to minimize the production time and costs, by telling a production facility when to make, with which staff, and on which equipment. Production scheduling aims to maximize the efficiency of the operation and reduce costs.
NCLEX	NCLEX is an examination for the licensing of nurses in the United States. There are two types, the NCLEX-RN and the NCLEX-PN. NCLEX examinations are developed and owned by the National Council of State Boards of Nursing, Inc. (NCSBN).
Procrastination	In psychology, procrastination refers to the act of replacing high-priority actions with tasks of lower priority, or doing something from which one derives enjoyment, and thus putting off important tasks to a later time. In accordance with Freud, the Pleasure principle may be responsible for procrastination; humans do not prefer negative emotions, and handing off a stressful task until a further date is enjoyable. The concept that humans work best under pressure provides additional enjoyment and motivation to postponing a task.
Adverse effect	In medicine, an adverse effect is a harmful and undesired effect resulting from a medication or other intervention such as surgery. An adverse effect may be termed a 'side effect', when judged to be secondary to a main or therapeutic effect. If it results from an unsuitable or incorrect dosage or procedure, this is called a medical error and not a complication.
Energy level	A quantum mechanical system or particle that is bound -- that is, confined spatially--can only take on certain discrete values of energy. This contrasts with classical particles, which can have any energy. These discrete values are called energy levels.
Estrogen	Estrogens (AmE), oestrogens (BE), or œstrogens, are a group of compounds named for their importance in the estrous cycle of humans and other animals. They are the primary female sex hormones. Natural estrogens are steroid hormones, while some synthetic ones are non-steroidal.

2. Developing Study Skills

Self-assessment	In social psychology, self-assessment is the process of looking at oneself in order to assess aspects that are important to one's identity. It is one of the motives that drive self-evaluation, along with self-verification and self-enhancement. Sedikides (1993) suggests that the self-assessment motive will prompt people to seek information to confirm their uncertain self-concept rather than their certain self-concept and at the same time people use self-assessment to enhance their certainty of their own self-knowledge.
ABC	ABC and its variations are initialism mnemonics for essential steps used by both medical professionals and lay persons (such as first aiders) when dealing with a patient. In its original form it stands for Airway, Breathing and Circulation. The protocol was originally developed as a memory aid for rescuers performing cardiopulmonary resuscitation, and the most widely known use of the initialism is in the care of the unconscious or unresponsive patient, although it is also used as a reminder of the priorities for assessment and treatment of patients in many acute medical and trauma situations, from first-aid to hospital medical treatment.
Electrolyte	An electrolyte is a liquid or gel that contains ions and can be decomposed by electrolysis, e.g., that present in a battery.

Commonly, electrolytes are solutions of acids, bases, or salts. Furthermore, some gases may act as electrolytes under conditions of high temperature or low pressure. |
| Nursing school | A nursing school is a type of educational institution, or part thereof, providing education and training to become a fully qualified nurse. The nature of nursing education and nursing qualifications varies considerably across the world. |
| Sims' position | The Sims' position is usually used for rectal examination, treatments and enemas. It is performed by having a patient lie on their left side, left hip and lower extremity straight, and right hip and knee bent. It is also called lateral recumbent position. |
| Content | Sigmund Freud, in his book The Interpretation of Dreams, suggested what he believed was 'the most valuable of all the discoveries it has been my good fortune to make.' Dreams allow a psychic safety net to be created that lets out feelings that may or may not be against the norm. Freud defines a dream's manifest content as a censored, figurative interpretation of its latent content, which includes senseless desires that would be inappropriate if conveyed directly.

Manifest content is the content of a dream as it is recalled by the dreamer in psychoanalysis. |
| Monoamine | Monoamine neurotransmitters are neurotransmitters and neuromodulators that contain one amino group that is connected to an aromatic ring by a two-carbon chain ($-CH_2-CH_2-$). All monoamines are derived from aromatic amino acids like phenylalanine, tyrosine, tryptophan, and the thyroid hormones by the action of aromatic amino acid decarboxylase enzymes. |

Monoamine oxidase	L-Monoamine oxidases (MAO) (EC 1.4.3.4) are a family of enzymes that catalyze the oxidation of monoamines. They are found bound to the outer membrane of mitochondria in most cell types in the body. The enzyme was originally discovered by Mary Bernheim in the liver and was named tyramine oxidase.
Oxidase	An oxidase is any enzyme that catalyzes an oxidation-reduction reaction involving molecular oxygen (O_2) as the electron acceptor. In these reactions, oxygen is reduced to water (H_2O) or hydrogen peroxide (H_2O_2). The oxidases are a subclass of the oxidoreductases.
Critical thinking	Critical thinking is reflective reasoning about beliefs and actions. It is a way of deciding whether a claim is always true, sometimes true, partly true, or false. Critical thinking can be traced in Western thought to the Socratic method of Ancient Greece and in the East, to the Buddhist kalama sutta and Abhidharma.

CHAPTER QUIZ: KEY TERMS, PEOPLE, PLACES, CONCEPTS

1. In social psychology, _____ is the process of looking at oneself in order to assess aspects that are important to one's identity. It is one of the motives that drive self-evaluation, along with self-verification and self-enhancement. Sedikides (1993) suggests that the _____ motive will prompt people to seek information to confirm their uncertain self-concept rather than their certain self-concept and at the same time people use _____ to enhance their certainty of their own self-knowledge.

   a. Self-assessment
   b. Single-subject design
   c. Single-subject research
   d. Six Sigma

2. _____ is an examination for the licensing of nurses in the United States. There are two types, the _____-RN and the _____-PN.

   _____ examinations are developed and owned by the National Council of State Boards of Nursing, Inc. (NCSBN).

   a. Nightingale Pledge
   b. Nightingale ward
   c. Notes on Nursing
   d. NCLEX

3. . In medicine, an _____ is a harmful and undesired effect resulting from a medication or other intervention such as surgery.

An _____ may be termed a 'side effect', when judged to be secondary to a main or therapeutic effect. If it results from an unsuitable or incorrect dosage or procedure, this is called a medical error and not a complication.

a. Adverse effect
b. Interruption science
c. Aarhus University
d. Range anxiety

4. _____ is the act or process of planning and exercising conscious control over the amount of time spent on specific activities, especially to increase efficiency or productivity. _____ may be aided by a range of skills, tools, and techniques used to manage time when accomplishing specific tasks, projects and goals complying with a due date. This set encompasses a wide scope of activities, and these include planning, allocating, setting goals, delegation, analysis of time spent, monitoring, organizing, scheduling, and prioritizing.

a. Tissue fluid
b. Time management
c. Balanced Budget Act
d. Children's Health Insurance Program

5. An _____ is any enzyme that catalyzes an oxidation-reduction reaction involving molecular oxygen (O_2) as the electron acceptor. In these reactions, oxygen is reduced to water (H_2O) or hydrogen peroxide (H_2O_2).

The _____s are a subclass of the oxidoreductases.

a. Aarhus University
b. Oxidase
c. Association for Computing Machinery
d. Dream interpretation

1. a
2. d
3. a
4. b
5. b

You can take the complete Chapter Practice Test

for 2. Developing Study Skills
on all key terms, persons, places, and concepts.

Online 99 Cents

http://www.JustTheFacts101.com

Use www.JustTheFacts101.com for all your study needs

including Facts101's online interactive problem solving labs in

chemistry, statistics, mathematics, and more.

3. Reducing Test Anxiety

CHAPTER OUTLINE: KEY TERMS, PEOPLE, PLACES, CONCEPTS

	Test anxiety
	Anxiety
	Deep breathing
	NPH insulin
	Relaxation technique
	Insulin
	Estrogen

CHAPTER HIGHLIGHTS & NOTES: KEY TERMS, PEOPLE, PLACES, CONCEPTS

Test anxiety	Test anxiety is a combination of perceived physiological over arousal, feelings of worry and dread, self-depreciating thoughts, tension, and somatic symptoms that occur during test situations. It is a physiological condition in which people experience extreme stress, anxiety, and discomfort during and/or before taking a test. These responses can drastically hinder an individual's ability to perform well and negatively affects their social emotional and behavioural development and feelings about themselves and school.
Anxiety	Anxiety is a psychological and physiological state characterized by somatic, emotional, cognitive, and behavioral components. It is the displeasing feeling of fear and concern. The root meaning of the word anxiety is 'to vex or trouble'; in either presence or absence of psychological stress, anxiety can create feelings of fear, worry, uneasiness, and dread.
Deep breathing	Diaphragmatic breathing, abdominal breathing, belly breathing or deep breathing is breathing that is done by contracting the diaphragm, a muscle located horizontally between the chest cavity and stomach cavity. Air enters the lungs and the belly expands during this type of breathing. This deep breathing is marked by expansion of the abdomen rather than the chest when breathing.
NPH insulin	NPH insulin is an intermediate-acting insulin given to help control the blood sugar level of those with diabetes. NPH was created in 1936 when Nordisk formulated 'isophane' porcine insulin by adding neutral protamine to regular insulin.

3. Reducing Test Anxiety

Relaxation technique	A relaxation technique is any method, process, procedure, or activity that helps a person to relax; to attain a state of increased calmness; or otherwise reduce levels of anxiety, stress or anger. Relaxation techniques are often employed as one element of a wider stress management program and can decrease muscle tension, lower the blood pressure and slow heart and breath rates, among other health benefits. People respond to stress in different ways, namely, by becoming overwhelmed, depressed or both.
Insulin	Insulin is a peptide hormone, produced by beta cells of the pancreas, and is central to regulating carbohydrate and fat metabolism in the body. Insulin causes cells in the liver, skeletal muscles, and fat tissue to take up glucose from the blood. In the liver and skeletal muscles, glucose is stored as glycogen, and in adipocytes it is stored as triglycerides.
Estrogen	Estrogens (AmE), oestrogens (BE), or œstrogens, are a group of compounds named for their importance in the estrous cycle of humans and other animals. They are the primary female sex hormones. Natural estrogens are steroid hormones, while some synthetic ones are non-steroidal.

1. _____ is a psychological and physiological state characterized by somatic, emotional, cognitive, and behavioral components. It is the displeasing feeling of fear and concern. The root meaning of the word _____ is 'to vex or trouble'; in either presence or absence of psychological stress, _____ can create feelings of fear, worry, uneasiness, and dread.

   a. Anxiety
   b. Angst
   c. Anxiety and Depression Association of America
   d. Anxiety threshold

2. _____ is an intermediate-acting insulin given to help control the blood sugar level of those with diabetes. NPH was created in 1936 when Nordisk formulated 'isophane' porcine insulin by adding neutral protamine to regular insulin.

   This is a suspension of crystalline zinc insulin combined with the positively charged polypeptide, protamine.

   a. Tissue fluid
   b. NPH insulin
   c. Balanced Budget Act
   d. Anxiety threshold

3. _____ is a combination of perceived physiological over arousal, feelings of worry and dread, self-depreciating thoughts, tension, and somatic symptoms that occur during test situations. It is a physiological condition in which people experience extreme stress, anxiety, and discomfort during and/or before taking a test. These responses can drastically hinder an individual's ability to perform well and negatively affects their social emotional and behavioural development and feelings about themselves and school.

   a. Worry
   b. Test anxiety
   c. Schizotypal personality
   d. Schizotypal

4. Diaphragmatic breathing, abdominal breathing, belly breathing or _____ is breathing that is done by contracting the diaphragm, a muscle located horizontally between the chest cavity and stomach cavity. Air enters the lungs and the belly expands during this type of breathing.

   This _____ is marked by expansion of the abdomen rather than the chest when breathing.

   a. Hypoxic drive
   b. Deep breathing
   c. Common Intermediate Language
   d. Anxiety threshold

5. A _____ is any method, process, procedure, or activity that helps a person to relax; to attain a state of increased calmness; or otherwise reduce levels of anxiety, stress or anger. _____s are often employed as one element of a wider stress management program and can decrease muscle tension, lower the blood pressure and slow heart and breath rates, among other health benefits.

   People respond to stress in different ways, namely, by becoming overwhelmed, depressed or both.

   a. Shaping
   b. Subjective units of distress scale
   c. Relaxation technique
   d. Anxiety threshold

1. a
2. b
3. b
4. b
5. c

You can take the complete Chapter Practice Test

for 3. Reducing Test Anxiety
on all key terms, persons, places, and concepts.

Online 99 Cents

http://www.JustTheFacts101.com

Use www.JustTheFacts101.com for all your study needs

including Facts101's online interactive problem solving labs in

chemistry, statistics, mathematics, and more.

4. NCLEXe Preparation

	NCLEX
	Pharmacology
	Self-assessment
	Energy level
	Estrogen
	Nursing school
	Test anxiety
	Anxiety
	Scheduling

NCLEX

NCLEX is an examination for the licensing of nurses in the United States. There are two types, the NCLEX-RN and the NCLEX-PN.

NCLEX examinations are developed and owned by the National Council of State Boards of Nursing, Inc. (NCSBN).

Pharmacology

Pharmacology is the branch of medicine and biology concerned with the study of drug action, where a drug can be broadly defined as any man-made, natural, or endogenous (within the cell) molecule which exerts a biochemical and/or physiological effect on the cell, tissue, organ, or organism. More specifically, it is the study of the interactions that occur between a living organism and chemicals that affect normal or abnormal biochemical function. If substances have medicinal properties, they are considered pharmaceuticals.

Self-assessment

In social psychology, self-assessment is the process of looking at oneself in order to assess aspects that are important to one's identity. It is one of the motives that drive self-evaluation, along with self-verification and self-enhancement.

CHAPTER HIGHLIGHTS & NOTES: KEY TERMS, PEOPLE, PLACES, CONCEPTS

Energy level	A quantum mechanical system or particle that is bound -- that is, confined spatially--can only take on certain discrete values of energy. This contrasts with classical particles, which can have any energy. These discrete values are called energy levels.
Estrogen	Estrogens (AmE), oestrogens (BE), or œstrogens, are a group of compounds named for their importance in the estrous cycle of humans and other animals. They are the primary female sex hormones. Natural estrogens are steroid hormones, while some synthetic ones are non-steroidal.
Nursing school	A nursing school is a type of educational institution, or part thereof, providing education and training to become a fully qualified nurse. The nature of nursing education and nursing qualifications varies considerably across the world.
Test anxiety	Test anxiety is a combination of perceived physiological over arousal, feelings of worry and dread, self-depreciating thoughts, tension, and somatic symptoms that occur during test situations. It is a physiological condition in which people experience extreme stress, anxiety, and discomfort during and/or before taking a test. These responses can drastically hinder an individual's ability to perform well and negatively affects their social emotional and behavioural development and feelings about themselves and school.
Anxiety	Anxiety is a psychological and physiological state characterized by somatic, emotional, cognitive, and behavioral components. It is the displeasing feeling of fear and concern. The root meaning of the word anxiety is 'to vex or trouble'; in either presence or absence of psychological stress, anxiety can create feelings of fear, worry, uneasiness, and dread.
Scheduling	Scheduling is an important tool for manufacturing and engineering, where it can have a major impact on the productivity of a process. In manufacturing, the purpose of scheduling is to minimize the production time and costs, by telling a production facility when to make, with which staff, and on which equipment. Production scheduling aims to maximize the efficiency of the operation and reduce costs.

4. NCLEXe Preparation

1. _____ is an examination for the licensing of nurses in the United States. There are two types, the _____-RN and the _____-PN.

   _____ examinations are developed and owned by the National Council of State Boards of Nursing, Inc. (NCSBN).

   a. NCLEX
   b. Nightingale ward
   c. Notes on Nursing
   d. Nurse Licensure Compact

2. _____ is the branch of medicine and biology concerned with the study of drug action, where a drug can be broadly defined as any man-made, natural, or endogenous (within the cell) molecule which exerts a biochemical and/or physiological effect on the cell, tissue, organ, or organism. More specifically, it is the study of the interactions that occur between a living organism and chemicals that affect normal or abnormal biochemical function. If substances have medicinal properties, they are considered pharmaceuticals.

   a. Pharmacology
   b. Benzodiazepine
   c. Binding coefficient
   d. Binding selectivity

3. In social psychology, _____ is the process of looking at oneself in order to assess aspects that are important to one's identity. It is one of the motives that drive self-evaluation, along with self-verification and self-enhancement. Sedikides (1993) suggests that the _____ motive will prompt people to seek information to confirm their uncertain self-concept rather than their certain self-concept and at the same time people use _____ to enhance their certainty of their own self-knowledge.

   a. Separation test
   b. Single-subject design
   c. Single-subject research
   d. Self-assessment

4. _____ is a combination of perceived physiological over arousal, feelings of worry and dread, self-depreciating thoughts, tension, and somatic symptoms that occur during test situations. It is a physiological condition in which people experience extreme stress, anxiety, and discomfort during and/or before taking a test. These responses can drastically hinder an individual's ability to perform well and negatively affects their social emotional and behavioural development and feelings about themselves and school.

   a. Worry
   b. The Worry Trap
   c. Schizotypal personality
   d. Test anxiety

4. NCLEXe Preparation

5. A quantum mechanical system or particle that is bound -- that is, confined spatially--can only take on certain discrete values of energy. This contrasts with classical particles, which can have any energy. These discrete values are called _____s.

   a. Energy level
   b. Ionization energy
   c. Oxidation state
   d. Six Sigma

1. a

2. a

3. d

4. d

5. a

You can take the complete Chapter Practice Test

for 4. NCLEXe Preparation
on all key terms, persons, places, and concepts.

Online 99 Cents

http://www.JustTheFacts101.com

Use www.JustTheFacts101.com for all your study needs

including Facts101's online interactive problem solving labs in

chemistry, statistics, mathematics, and more.

5. Alternate Item Formats

CHAPTER OUTLINE: KEY TERMS, PEOPLE, PLACES, CONCEPTS

	ABC
	Maslow's hierarchy of needs
	Nursing process

CHAPTER HIGHLIGHTS & NOTES: KEY TERMS, PEOPLE, PLACES, CONCEPTS

ABC	ABC and its variations are initialism mnemonics for essential steps used by both medical professionals and lay persons (such as first aiders) when dealing with a patient. In its original form it stands for Airway, Breathing and Circulation. The protocol was originally developed as a memory aid for rescuers performing cardiopulmonary resuscitation, and the most widely known use of the initialism is in the care of the unconscious or unresponsive patient, although it is also used as a reminder of the priorities for assessment and treatment of patients in many acute medical and trauma situations, from first-aid to hospital medical treatment.
Maslow's hierarchy of needs	Maslow's hierarchy of needs is a theory in psychology proposed by Abraham Maslow in his 1943 paper 'A Theory of Human Motivation'. Maslow subsequently extended the idea to include his observations of humans' innate curiosity. His theories parallel many other theories of human developmental psychology, some of which focus on describing the stages of growth in humans.
Nursing process	The nursing process is a modified scientific method. Nursing practise was first described as a four stage nursing process by Ida Jean Orlando in 1958. It should not be confused with nursing theories or Health informatics. The diagnosis phase was added later.

5. Alternate Item Formats

1. The _____ is a modified scientific method. Nursing practise was first described as a four stage _____ by Ida Jean Orlando in 1958. It should not be confused with nursing theories or Health informatics. The diagnosis phase was added later.

   a. Nursing process
   b. nurse-midwives
   c. Tissue fluid
   d. Emergency medical systems operator

2. _____ and its variations are initialism mnemonics for essential steps used by both medical professionals and lay persons (such as first aiders) when dealing with a patient. In its original form it stands for Airway, Breathing and Circulation. The protocol was originally developed as a memory aid for rescuers performing cardiopulmonary resuscitation, and the most widely known use of the initialism is in the care of the unconscious or unresponsive patient, although it is also used as a reminder of the priorities for assessment and treatment of patients in many acute medical and trauma situations, from first-aid to hospital medical treatment.

   a. ABC
   b. Ambulance station
   c. Emergency medical dispatcher
   d. Emergency medical systems operator

3. _____ is a theory in psychology proposed by Abraham Maslow in his 1943 paper 'A Theory of Human Motivation'. Maslow subsequently extended the idea to include his observations of humans' innate curiosity. His theories parallel many other theories of human developmental psychology, some of which focus on describing the stages of growth in humans.

   a. Maslow's hierarchy of needs
   b. Ambulance station
   c. Emergency medical dispatcher
   d. Emergency medical systems operator

1. a

2. a

3. a

You can take the complete Chapter Practice Test

for 5. Alternate Item Formats
on all key terms, persons, places, and concepts.

Online 99 Cents

http://www.JustTheFacts101.com

Use www.JustTheFacts101.com for all your study needs

including Facts101's online interactive problem solving labs in

chemistry, statistics, mathematics, and more.

6. How to Avoid Reading into the Question

CHAPTER OUTLINE: KEY TERMS, PEOPLE, PLACES, CONCEPTS

	Carbonic anhydrase
	Pharmacology
	Content
	Survivors guilt

CHAPTER HIGHLIGHTS & NOTES: KEY TERMS, PEOPLE, PLACES, CONCEPTS

Carbonic anhydrase

The carbonic anhydrases (or carbonate dehydratases) form a family of enzymes that catalyze the rapid interconversion of carbon dioxide and water to bicarbonate and protons (or vice-versa), a reversible reaction that occurs rather slowly in the absence of a catalyst. The active site of most carbonic anhydrases contains a zinc ion; they are therefore classified as metalloenzymes.

One of the functions of the enzyme in animals is to interconvert carbon dioxide and bicarbonate to maintain acid-base balance in blood and other tissues, and to help transport carbon dioxide out of tissues.

Pharmacology

Pharmacology is the branch of medicine and biology concerned with the study of drug action, where a drug can be broadly defined as any man-made, natural, or endogenous (within the cell) molecule which exerts a biochemical and/or physiological effect on the cell, tissue, organ, or organism. More specifically, it is the study of the interactions that occur between a living organism and chemicals that affect normal or abnormal biochemical function. If substances have medicinal properties, they are considered pharmaceuticals.

Content

Sigmund Freud, in his book The Interpretation of Dreams, suggested what he believed was 'the most valuable of all the discoveries it has been my good fortune to make.' Dreams allow a psychic safety net to be created that lets out feelings that may or may not be against the norm. Freud defines a dream's manifest content as a censored, figurative interpretation of its latent content, which includes senseless desires that would be inappropriate if conveyed directly.

Manifest content is the content of a dream as it is recalled by the dreamer in psychoanalysis.

Survivors guilt

Survivor, survivor's, or survivors guilt is a mental condition that occurs when a person perceives themselves to have done wrong by surviving a traumatic event when others did not.

6. How to Avoid Reading into the Question

It may be found among survivors of combat, natural disasters, epidemics, among the friends and family of those who have committed suicide, and in non-mortal situations such as among those whose colleagues are laid off. The experience and manifestation of survivor's guilt will depend on an individual's psychological profile.

1. The _____s (or carbonate dehydratases) form a family of enzymes that catalyze the rapid interconversion of carbon dioxide and water to bicarbonate and protons (or vice-versa), a reversible reaction that occurs rather slowly in the absence of a catalyst. The active site of most _____s contains a zinc ion; they are therefore classified as metalloenzymes.

   One of the functions of the enzyme in animals is to interconvert carbon dioxide and bicarbonate to maintain acid-base balance in blood and other tissues, and to help transport carbon dioxide out of tissues.

   a. Digestive enzyme
   b. Dipeptidase
   c. Steapsin
   d. Carbonic anhydrase

2. Survivor, survivor's, or _____ is a mental condition that occurs when a person perceives themselves to have done wrong by surviving a traumatic event when others did not. It may be found among survivors of combat, natural disasters, epidemics, among the friends and family of those who have committed suicide, and in non-mortal situations such as among those whose colleagues are laid off. The experience and manifestation of survivor's guilt will depend on an individual's psychological profile.

   a. Zero stroke
   b. Depression
   c. Dissociation
   d. Survivors guilt

3. . Sigmund Freud, in his book The Interpretation of Dreams, suggested what he believed was 'the most valuable of all the discoveries it has been my good fortune to make.' Dreams allow a psychic safety net to be created that lets out feelings that may or may not be against the norm. Freud defines a dream's manifest _____ as a censored, figurative interpretation of its latent _____, which includes senseless desires that would be inappropriate if conveyed directly.

   Manifest _____ is the _____ of a dream as it is recalled by the dreamer in psychoanalysis.

   a. Death drive

b. Destrudo

c. Content

d. Dream interpretation

4. _____ is the branch of medicine and biology concerned with the study of drug action, where a drug can be broadly defined as any man-made, natural, or endogenous (within the cell) molecule which exerts a biochemical and/or physiological effect on the cell, tissue, organ, or organism. More specifically, it is the study of the interactions that occur between a living organism and chemicals that affect normal or abnormal biochemical function. If substances have medicinal properties, they are considered pharmaceuticals.

a. Bencao Gangmu

b. Benzodiazepine

c. Binding coefficient

d. Pharmacology

1. d
2. d
3. c
4. d

You can take the complete Chapter Practice Test

for 6. How to Avoid Reading into the Question
on all key terms, persons, places, and concepts.

Online 99 Cents

http://www.JustTheFacts101.com

Use www.JustTheFacts101.com for all your study needs

including Facts101's online interactive problem solving labs in

chemistry, statistics, mathematics, and more.

7. Positive and Negative Event Queries

CHAPTER OUTLINE: KEY TERMS, PEOPLE, PLACES, CONCEPTS

	NCLEX
	Pharmacology

CHAPTER HIGHLIGHTS & NOTES: KEY TERMS, PEOPLE, PLACES, CONCEPTS

NCLEX	NCLEX is an examination for the licensing of nurses in the United States. There are two types, the NCLEX-RN and the NCLEX-PN. NCLEX examinations are developed and owned by the National Council of State Boards of Nursing, Inc. (NCSBN).
Pharmacology	Pharmacology is the branch of medicine and biology concerned with the study of drug action, where a drug can be broadly defined as any man-made, natural, or endogenous (within the cell) molecule which exerts a biochemical and/or physiological effect on the cell, tissue, organ, or organism. More specifically, it is the study of the interactions that occur between a living organism and chemicals that affect normal or abnormal biochemical function. If substances have medicinal properties, they are considered pharmaceuticals.

CHAPTER QUIZ: KEY TERMS, PEOPLE, PLACES, CONCEPTS

1. _____ is an examination for the licensing of nurses in the United States. There are two types, the _____-RN and the _____-PN.

    _____ examinations are developed and owned by the National Council of State Boards of Nursing, Inc. (NCSBN).

    a. Nightingale Pledge
    b. NCLEX
    c. Notes on Nursing
    d. Nurse Licensure Compact

2. _____ is the branch of medicine and biology concerned with the study of drug action, where a drug can be broadly defined as any man-made, natural, or endogenous (within the cell) molecule which exerts a biochemical and/or physiological effect on the cell, tissue, organ, or organism. More specifically, it is the study of the interactions that occur between a living organism and chemicals that affect normal or abnormal biochemical function. If substances have medicinal properties, they are considered pharmaceuticals.

a. Bencao Gangmu
b. Pharmacology
c. Binding coefficient
d. Binding selectivity

1. b
2. b

You can take the complete Chapter Practice Test

for 7. Positive and Negative Event Queries
on all key terms, persons, places, and concepts.

Online 99 Cents

http://www.JustTheFacts101.com

Use www.JustTheFacts101.com for all your study needs

including Facts101's online interactive problem solving labs in

chemistry, statistics, mathematics, and more.

8. Questions Requiring Prioritization

CHAPTER OUTLINE: KEY TERMS, PEOPLE, PLACES, CONCEPTS

	Priority level
	Scheduling
	ABC
	Nursing process
	Phenothiazine
	Estrogen

CHAPTER HIGHLIGHTS & NOTES: KEY TERMS, PEOPLE, PLACES, CONCEPTS

Priority level	Priority level, in the Telecommunications Service Priority system, is the level that may be assigned to an NS/EP telecommunications service, which level specifies the order in which provisioning or restoration of the service is to occur relative to other NS/EP or non-NS/EP telecommunication services. Priority levels authorized are designated (highest to lowest) 'E,' '1,' '2,' '3,' '4,' and '5' for provisioning and '1,' '2,' '3,' '4,' and '5' for restoration.
Scheduling	Scheduling is an important tool for manufacturing and engineering, where it can have a major impact on the productivity of a process. In manufacturing, the purpose of scheduling is to minimize the production time and costs, by telling a production facility when to make, with which staff, and on which equipment. Production scheduling aims to maximize the efficiency of the operation and reduce costs.
ABC	ABC and its variations are initialism mnemonics for essential steps used by both medical professionals and lay persons (such as first aiders) when dealing with a patient. In its original form it stands for Airway, Breathing and Circulation. The protocol was originally developed as a memory aid for rescuers performing cardiopulmonary resuscitation, and the most widely known use of the initialism is in the care of the unconscious or unresponsive patient, although it is also used as a reminder of the priorities for assessment and treatment of patients in many acute medical and trauma situations, from first-aid to hospital medical treatment.
Nursing process	The nursing process is a modified scientific method.

8. Questions Requiring Prioritization

	Nursing practise was first described as a four stage nursing process by Ida Jean Orlando in 1958. It should not be confused with nursing theories or Health informatics. The diagnosis phase was added later.
Phenothiazine	Phenothiazine is an organic compound that occurs in various antipsychotic and antihistaminic drugs. It has the formula $S(C_6H_4)_2NH$. This yellow tricyclic compound is soluble in acetic acid, benzene, and ether. The compound is related to the thiazine-class of heterocyclic compounds. The phenothiazine structure occurs in various neuroleptic drugs, e.g. chlorpromazine, and antihistaminic drugs, e.g. promethazine. The term 'phenothiazines' describes the largest of the five main classes of neuroleptic antipsychotic drugs. These drugs have antipsychotic and, often, antiemetic properties, although they may also cause severe side effects such as extrapyramidal symptoms (including akathisia and tardive dyskinesia), hyperprolactinaemia, and the rare but potentially fatal neuroleptic malignant syndrome as well as substantial weight gain.
Estrogen	Estrogens (AmE), oestrogens (BE), or œstrogens, are a group of compounds named for their importance in the estrous cycle of humans and other animals. They are the primary female sex hormones. Natural estrogens are steroid hormones, while some synthetic ones are non-steroidal.

1. _____s (AmE), o_____s (BE), or œstrogens, are a group of compounds named for their importance in the estrous cycle of humans and other animals. They are the primary female sex hormones. Natural _____s are steroid hormones, while some synthetic ones are non-steroidal.

   a. External sphincter muscle of female urethra
   b. External urethral orifice
   c. Interlabial sulci
   d. Estrogen

2. The _____ is a modified scientific method. Nursing practise was first described as a four stage _____ by Ida Jean Orlando in 1958. It should not be confused with nursing theories or Health informatics. The diagnosis phase was added later.

   a. Nursing diagnoses
   b. nurse-midwives
   c. Tissue fluid
   d. Nursing process

3. _____ and its variations are initialism mnemonics for essential steps used by both medical professionals and lay persons (such as first aiders) when dealing with a patient. In its original form it stands for Airway, Breathing and Circulation. The protocol was originally developed as a memory aid for rescuers performing cardiopulmonary resuscitation, and the most widely known use of the initialism is in the care of the unconscious or unresponsive patient, although it is also used as a reminder of the priorities for assessment and treatment of patients in many acute medical and trauma situations, from first-aid to hospital medical treatment.

a. Advanced cardiac life support
b. Ambulance station
c. ABC
d. Emergency medical systems operator

4. _____, in the Telecommunications Service Priority system, is the level that may be assigned to an NS/EP telecommunications service, which level specifies the order in which provisioning or restoration of the service is to occur relative to other NS/EP or non-NS/EP telecommunication services.

_____s authorized are designated (highest to lowest) 'E,' '1,' '2,' '3,' '4,' and '5' for provisioning and '1,' '2,' '3,' '4,' and '5' for restoration.

a. Priority level
b. Red Cross parcel
c. Robocup Rescue Simulation
d. Rohn Emergency Scale

5. _____ is an important tool for manufacturing and engineering, where it can have a major impact on the productivity of a process. In manufacturing, the purpose of _____ is to minimize the production time and costs, by telling a production facility when to make, with which staff, and on which equipment. Production _____ aims to maximize the efficiency of the operation and reduce costs.

a. School timetable
b. Strategic communication
c. Succession planning
d. Scheduling

1. d
2. d
3. c
4. a
5. d

You can take the complete Chapter Practice Test

for 8. Questions Requiring Prioritization
on all key terms, persons, places, and concepts.

Online 99 Cents

http://www.JustTheFacts101.com

Use www.JustTheFacts101.com for all your study needs

including Facts101's online interactive problem solving labs in

chemistry, statistics, mathematics, and more.

9. Leading and Managing, Delegating, and Assignment-Making Questions

	Practical nurse
	Adverse effect
	Nursing process
	Internship
	Nursing school
	Electrolyte
	Registered nurse
	Time management

CHAPTER HIGHLIGHTS & NOTES: KEY TERMS, PEOPLE, PLACES, CONCEPTS

Practical nurse	A licensed practical nurse in much of the United States and most Canadian provinces is a nurse who cares for people who are sick, injured, convalescent, or disabled under the direction of registered nurses and physicians. In the U.S. states of California and Texas they are called licensed vocational nurse (LVN). Equivalent professions outside the United States are 'registered practical nurse' (RPNs) in the Canadian province of Ontario, 'enrolled nurses' (ENs) or 'Division 2 nurses' in Australia and New Zealand, and 'state enrolled nurses' (SENs) in the United Kingdom.
Adverse effect	In medicine, an adverse effect is a harmful and undesired effect resulting from a medication or other intervention such as surgery. An adverse effect may be termed a 'side effect', when judged to be secondary to a main or therapeutic effect. If it results from an unsuitable or incorrect dosage or procedure, this is called a medical error and not a complication.
Nursing process	The nursing process is a modified scientific method. Nursing practise was first described as a four stage nursing process by Ida Jean Orlando in 1958. It should not be confused with nursing theories or Health informatics.

Internship	A medical intern is a term used in the United States for a physician in training who has completed medical school. An intern has a medical degree, but does not have a full license to practice medicine unsupervised. In other countries medical education generally ends with a period of practical training similar to internship, but the way the overall program of academic and practical medical training is structured differs in each case, as does the terminology used .
Nursing school	A nursing school is a type of educational institution, or part thereof, providing education and training to become a fully qualified nurse. The nature of nursing education and nursing qualifications varies considerably across the world.
Electrolyte	An electrolyte is a liquid or gel that contains ions and can be decomposed by electrolysis, e.g., that present in a battery. Commonly, electrolytes are solutions of acids, bases, or salts. Furthermore, some gases may act as electrolytes under conditions of high temperature or low pressure.
Registered nurse	A registered nurse is a nurse who has graduated from a nursing program at a college or university and has passed a national licensing exam. Registered nurses help individuals, families, and groups to achieve health and prevent disease. They care for the sick and injured in hospitals and other health care facilities, physicians' offices, private homes, public health agencies, schools, camps, and industry.
Time management	Time management is the act or process of planning and exercising conscious control over the amount of time spent on specific activities, especially to increase efficiency or productivity. Time management may be aided by a range of skills, tools, and techniques used to manage time when accomplishing specific tasks, projects and goals complying with a due date. This set encompasses a wide scope of activities, and these include planning, allocating, setting goals, delegation, analysis of time spent, monitoring, organizing, scheduling, and prioritizing.

9. Leading and Managing, Delegating, and Assignment-Making Questions

1. A licensed _____ in much of the United States and most Canadian provinces is a nurse who cares for people who are sick, injured, convalescent, or disabled under the direction of registered nurses and physicians. In the U.S. states of California and Texas they are called licensed vocational nurse (LVN).

   Equivalent professions outside the United States are 'registered _____' (RPNs) in the Canadian province of Ontario, 'enrolled nurses' (ENs) or 'Division 2 nurses' in Australia and New Zealand, and 'state enrolled nurses' (SENs) in the United Kingdom.

   a. Tissue fluid
   b. Practical nurse
   c. Balanced Budget Act
   d. Children's Health Insurance Program

2. _____ is the act or process of planning and exercising conscious control over the amount of time spent on specific activities, especially to increase efficiency or productivity. _____ may be aided by a range of skills, tools, and techniques used to manage time when accomplishing specific tasks, projects and goals complying with a due date. This set encompasses a wide scope of activities, and these include planning, allocating, setting goals, delegation, analysis of time spent, monitoring, organizing, scheduling, and prioritizing.

   a. Time management
   b. Women's Health Care Nurse Practitioner
   c. Licensed vocational nurse
   d. practical nurse

3. A _____ is a nurse who has graduated from a nursing program at a college or university and has passed a national licensing exam. _____s help individuals, families, and groups to achieve health and prevent disease. They care for the sick and injured in hospitals and other health care facilities, physicians' offices, private homes, public health agencies, schools, camps, and industry.

   a. Registered nurse
   b. Women's Health Care Nurse Practitioner
   c. Licensed vocational nurse
   d. practical nurse

4. . An _____ is a liquid or gel that contains ions and can be decomposed by electrolysis, e.g., that present in a battery.

   Commonly, _____s are solutions of acids, bases, or salts. Furthermore, some gases may act as _____s under conditions of high temperature or low pressure.

   a. Enzyme multiplied immunoassay technique
   b. Erythrocyte sedimentation rate
   c. Euglobulin lysis time

5. In medicine, an _____ is a harmful and undesired effect resulting from a medication or other intervention such as surgery.

    An _____ may be termed a 'side effect', when judged to be secondary to a main or therapeutic effect. If it results from an unsuitable or incorrect dosage or procedure, this is called a medical error and not a complication.

    a. ECRI Institute
    b. Adverse effect
    c. Aarhus University
    d. Association for Computing Machinery

1. b
2. a
3. a
4. d
5. b

You can take the complete Chapter Practice Test

for 9. Leading and Managing, Delegating, and Assignment-Making Questions
on all key terms, persons, places, and concepts.

Online 99 Cents

http://www.JustTheFacts101.com

Use www.JustTheFacts101.com for all your study needs

including Facts101's online interactive problem solving labs in

chemistry, statistics, mathematics, and more.

10. Communication Questions

CHAPTER OUTLINE: KEY TERMS, PEOPLE, PLACES, CONCEPTS

	Coagulation
	NCLEX
	Nurse-client relationship
	End-of-life care

CHAPTER HIGHLIGHTS & NOTES: KEY TERMS, PEOPLE, PLACES, CONCEPTS

Coagulation	Coagulation is the process by which blood forms clots. It is an important part of hemostasis, the cessation of blood loss from a damaged vessel, wherein a damaged blood vessel wall is covered by a platelet and fibrin-containing clot to stop bleeding and begin repair of the damaged vessel. Disorders of coagulation can lead to an increased risk of bleeding (hemorrhage) or obstructive clotting (thrombosis).
NCLEX	NCLEX is an examination for the licensing of nurses in the United States. There are two types, the NCLEX-RN and the NCLEX-PN. NCLEX examinations are developed and owned by the National Council of State Boards of Nursing, Inc. (NCSBN).
Nurse-client relationship	The nurse-client relationship in Hildegard E. Peplau's Interpersonal Relations Model theory is essential to nursing practice. It is the nurse-client interaction that is toward enhancing the client's well-being, and the client may be an individual, a family, a group or a community. Peplau thought the basic element of the relationship is what goes on between the nurse and patient (Interpersonal Theory 5).
End-of-life care	In medicine, end-of-life care refers to medical care not only of patients in the final hours or days of their lives, but more broadly, medical care of all those with a terminal illness or terminal condition that has become advanced, progressive and incurable. Regarding cancer care the United States National Cancer Institute writes:' When a patient's health care team determines that the cancer can no longer be controlled, medical testing and cancer treatment often stop. But the patient's care continues.'

10. Communication Questions

1. _____ is the process by which blood forms clots. It is an important part of hemostasis, the cessation of blood loss from a damaged vessel, wherein a damaged blood vessel wall is covered by a platelet and fibrin-containing clot to stop bleeding and begin repair of the damaged vessel. Disorders of _____ can lead to an increased risk of bleeding (hemorrhage) or obstructive clotting (thrombosis).

    a. Cofact
    b. Coagulation
    c. Factor IX
    d. Factor V

2. The _____ in Hildegard E. Peplau's Interpersonal Relations Model theory is essential to nursing practice. It is the nurse-client interaction that is toward enhancing the client's well-being, and the client may be an individual, a family, a group or a community. Peplau thought the basic element of the relationship is what goes on between the nurse and patient (Interpersonal Theory 5).

    a. Nurse-client relationship
    b. Nightingale ward
    c. Notes on Nursing
    d. Nurse Licensure Compact

3. _____ is an examination for the licensing of nurses in the United States. There are two types, the _____-RN and the _____-PN.

    _____ examinations are developed and owned by the National Council of State Boards of Nursing, Inc. (NCSBN).

    a. Nightingale Pledge
    b. NCLEX
    c. Notes on Nursing
    d. Nurse Licensure Compact

4. In medicine, _____ refers to medical care not only of patients in the final hours or days of their lives, but more broadly, medical care of all those with a terminal illness or terminal condition that has become advanced, progressive and incurable.

    Regarding cancer care the United States National Cancer Institute writes:'

    When a patient's health care team determines that the cancer can no longer be controlled, medical testing and cancer treatment often stop. But the patient's care continues.'

    a. Errol Solomon Meyers Memorial Lecture
    b. End-of-life care
    c. Exercise prescription
    d. Exercise prescription software

ANSWER KEY
10. Communication Questions

1. b
2. a
3. b
4. b

You can take the complete Chapter Practice Test

for 10. Communication Questions
on all key terms, persons, places, and concepts.

Online 99 Cents

http://www.JustTheFacts101.com

Use www.JustTheFacts101.com for all your study needs

including Facts101's online interactive problem solving labs in

chemistry, statistics, mathematics, and more.

11. Pharmacology, Medication, and Intravenous Calculation Questions

CHAPTER OUTLINE: KEY TERMS, PEOPLE, PLACES, CONCEPTS

NCLEX

Pharmacology

Adverse effect

Insulin

Morphine

Toxic effects

End-of-life care

Antihistamine

Side effect

Anaphylaxis

Digoxin

Furosemide

Lasix

Medical terminology

Androgen

Angiotensin-converting enzyme

Antidiuretic

Antidiuretic hormone

Benzodiazepine

Calcium

Calcium channel

	Channel blocker
	Enzyme
	Hormone
	Carbonic anhydrase
	Corticosteroid
	Estrogen
	Glucocorticoid
	Phenothiazine
	Proton
	Proton pump
	Sulfonylurea
	Thiazide
	Thyroid
	Thyroid hormone
	Diuretic
	Receptor antagonist
	Intravenous
	Histamine

NCLEX	NCLEX is an examination for the licensing of nurses in the United States. There are two types, the NCLEX-RN and the NCLEX-PN.
	NCLEX examinations are developed and owned by the National Council of State Boards of Nursing, Inc. (NCSBN).
Pharmacology	Pharmacology is the branch of medicine and biology concerned with the study of drug action, where a drug can be broadly defined as any man-made, natural, or endogenous (within the cell) molecule which exerts a biochemical and/or physiological effect on the cell, tissue, organ, or organism. More specifically, it is the study of the interactions that occur between a living organism and chemicals that affect normal or abnormal biochemical function. If substances have medicinal properties, they are considered pharmaceuticals.
Adverse effect	In medicine, an adverse effect is a harmful and undesired effect resulting from a medication or other intervention such as surgery.
	An adverse effect may be termed a 'side effect', when judged to be secondary to a main or therapeutic effect. If it results from an unsuitable or incorrect dosage or procedure, this is called a medical error and not a complication.
Insulin	Insulin is a peptide hormone, produced by beta cells of the pancreas, and is central to regulating carbohydrate and fat metabolism in the body. Insulin causes cells in the liver, skeletal muscles, and fat tissue to take up glucose from the blood. In the liver and skeletal muscles, glucose is stored as glycogen, and in adipocytes it is stored as triglycerides.
Morphine	Morphine (; MS Contin, MSIR, Avinza, Kadian, Oramorph, Roxanol, Kapanol) is a potent opiate analgesic drug that is used to relieve severe pain. It was first isolated in 1804 by Friedrich Sertürner, first distributed by him in 1817, and first commercially sold by Merck in 1827, which at the time was a single small chemists' shop. It was more widely used after the invention of the hypodermic needle in 1857. It took its name from the Greek god of dreams Morpheus .
Toxic effects	Toxicity is the degree to which a substance can damage an organism. Toxicity can refer to the effect on a whole organism, such as an animal, bacterium, or plant, as well as the effect on a substructure of the organism, such as a cell (cytotoxicity) or an organ such as the liver (hepatotoxicity). By extension, the word may be metaphorically used to describe toxic effects on larger and more complex groups, such as the family unit or society at large.
End-of-life care	In medicine, end-of-life care refers to medical care not only of patients in the final hours or days of their lives, but more broadly, medical care of all those with a terminal illness or terminal condition that has become advanced, progressive and incurable.
	Regarding cancer care the United States National Cancer Institute writes:'

11. Pharmacology, Medication, and Intravenous Calculation Questions

	When a patient's health care team determines that the cancer can no longer be controlled, medical testing and cancer treatment often stop. But the patient's care continues.'
Antihistamine	A histamine antagonist (commonly called an antihistamine) is a pharmaceutical drug that inhibits the action of histamine by either blocking its attachment to histamine receptors, or inhibiting the enzymatic activity of histidine decarboxylase; catalyzing the transformation of histidine into histamine . It is commonly used for the relief of allergies caused by intolerance of proteins.
Side effect	In medicine, a side effect is an effect, whether therapeutic or adverse, that is secondary to the one intended; although the term is predominantly employed to describe adverse effects, it can also apply to beneficial, but unintended, consequences of the use of a drug. Occasionally, drugs are prescribed or procedures performed specifically for their side effects; in that case, said side effect ceases to be a side effect, and is now an intended effect. For instance, X-rays were historically (and are currently) used as an imaging technique; the discovery of their oncolytic capability led to their employ in radiotherapy (ablation of malignant tumours).
Anaphylaxis	Anaphylaxis is a serious allergic reaction that is rapid in onset and may cause death. It typically causes a number of symptoms including an itchy rash, throat swelling, and low blood pressure. Common causes include insect bites/stings, foods, and medications.
Digoxin	Digoxin INN () is a purified cardiac glycoside and extracted from the foxglove plant, Digitalis lanata. Its corresponding aglycone is digoxigenin, and its acetyl derivative is acetyldigoxin. Digoxin is widely used in the treatment of various heart conditions, namely atrial fibrillation, atrial flutter and sometimes heart failure that cannot be controlled by other medication.
Furosemide	Furosemide or frusemide (former BAN) is a loop diuretic used in the treatment of congestive heart failure and edema. It is most commonly marketed by Sanofi-Aventis under the brand name Lasix. It has also been used to prevent Thoroughbred and Standardbred race horses from bleeding through the nose during races.
Lasix	Furosemide or frusemide (former BAN) is a loop diuretic used in the treatment of congestive heart failure and edema. It is most commonly marketed by Sanofi under the brand name Lasix, and also under the brand names Fusid and Frumex. It has also been used to prevent Thoroughbred and Standardbred race horses from bleeding through the nose during races.
Medical terminology	Medical terminology is a language for accurately describing the human body and associated components, conditions, processes and process in a science-based manner. Some examples are: R.I.C.E., trapezius, and latissimus dorsi. It is to be used in the medical and nursing fields.

Androgen	Androgen, is the generic term for any natural or synthetic compound, usually a steroid hormone, that stimulates or controls the development and maintenance of male characteristics in vertebrates by binding to androgen receptors. This includes the activity of the accessory male sex organs and development of male secondary sex characteristics. Androgens were first discovered in 1936. Androgens are also the original anabolic steroids and the precursor of all estrogens, which are stress hormones.
Angiotensin-converting enzyme	Angiotensin-converting enzyme increases blood pressure by causing blood vessels to constrict. It does that by converting angiotensin I to angiotensin II, which constricts the vessels. For this reason, drugs known as Angiotensin converting enzyme inhibitors are used to lower blood pressure.
Antidiuretic	An antidiuretic is an agent or drug that, administered to an organism, helps control body water balance by reducing urination, opposing diuresis.
Antidiuretic hormone	Arginine vasopressin, also known as vasopressin, argipressin or antidiuretic hormone is a neurohypophysial hormone found in most mammals. Its two primary functions are to retain water in the body and to constrict blood vessels. Vasopressin regulates the body's retention of water by acting to increase water absorption in the collecting ducts of the kidney nephron.
Benzodiazepine	A benzodiazepine is a psychoactive drug whose core chemical structure is the fusion of a benzene ring and a diazepine ring. The first benzodiazepine, chlordiazepoxide (Librium), was discovered accidentally by Leo Sternbach in 1955, and made available in 1960 by Hoffmann-La Roche, which has also marketed diazepam (Valium) since 1963. Benzodiazepines enhance the effect of the neurotransmitter gamma-aminobutyric acid (GABA-A), resulting in sedative, hypnotic (sleep-inducing), anxiolytic (anti-anxiety), anticonvulsant, and muscle relaxant properties; also seen in the applied pharmacology of high doses of many shorter-acting benzodiazepines are amnesic-dissociative actions.
Calcium	Calcium is the chemical element with the symbol Ca and atomic number 20. It has an atomic mass of 40.078 amu. Calcium is a soft gray alkaline earth metal, and is the fifth-most-abundant element by mass in the Earth's crust. Calcium is also the fifth-most-abundant dissolved ion in seawater by both molarity and mass, after sodium, chloride, magnesium, and sulfate.
Calcium channel	A Calcium channel is an ion channel which displays selective permeability to calcium ions. It is sometimes synonymous as voltage-dependent calcium channel, although there are also ligand-gated calcium channels.

11. Pharmacology, Medication, and Intravenous Calculation Questions

Enzyme	Enzymes are large biological molecules responsible for the thousands of chemical interconversions that sustain life. They are highly selective catalysts, greatly accelerating both the rate and specificity of metabolic reactions, from the digestion of food to the synthesis of DNA. Most enzymes are proteins, although some catalytic RNA molecules have been identified. Enzymes adopt a specific three-dimensional structure, and may employ organic (e.g. biotin) and inorganic (e.g. magnesium ion) cofactors to assist in catalysis.
Hormone	A hormone is a chemical released by a cell or a gland in one part of the body that sends out messages that affect cells in other parts of the organism. Only a little amount of hormone is required to alter cell metabolism. In essence, it is a chemical messenger that transports a signal from one cell to another.
Carbonic anhydrase	The carbonic anhydrases (or carbonate dehydratases) form a family of enzymes that catalyze the rapid interconversion of carbon dioxide and water to bicarbonate and protons (or vice-versa), a reversible reaction that occurs rather slowly in the absence of a catalyst. The active site of most carbonic anhydrases contains a zinc ion; they are therefore classified as metalloenzymes. One of the functions of the enzyme in animals is to interconvert carbon dioxide and bicarbonate to maintain acid-base balance in blood and other tissues, and to help transport carbon dioxide out of tissues.
Corticosteroid	Corticosteroids are a class of steroid hormones that are produced in the adrenal cortex. Corticosteroids are involved in a wide range of physiologic systems such as stress response, immune response and regulation of inflammation, carbohydrate metabolism, protein catabolism, blood electrolyte levels, and behavior. •Glucocorticoids such as cortisol control carbohydrate, fat and protein metabolism and are anti-inflammatory by preventing phospholipid release, decreasing eosinophil action and a number of other mechanisms.•Mineralocorticoids such as aldosterone control electrolyte and water levels, mainly by promoting sodium retention in the kidney. Some common natural hormones are corticosterone ($C_{21}H_{30}O_4$), cortisone ($C_{21}H_{28}O_5$, 17-hydroxy-11-dehydrocorticosterone) and aldosterone.
Estrogen	Estrogens (AmE), oestrogens (BE), or œstrogens, are a group of compounds named for their importance in the estrous cycle of humans and other animals. They are the primary female sex hormones. Natural estrogens are steroid hormones, while some synthetic ones are non-steroidal.
Glucocorticoid	Glucocorticoids (GC) are a class of steroid hormones that bind to the glucocorticoid receptor (GR), which is present in almost every vertebrate animal cell. GCs are part of the feedback mechanism in the immune system that turns immune activity (inflammation) down.

Phenothiazine	Phenothiazine is an organic compound that occurs in various antipsychotic and antihistaminic drugs. It has the formula $S(C_6H_4)_2NH$. This yellow tricyclic compound is soluble in acetic acid, benzene, and ether. The compound is related to the thiazine-class of heterocyclic compounds.

The phenothiazine structure occurs in various neuroleptic drugs, e.g. chlorpromazine, and antihistaminic drugs, e.g. promethazine. The term 'phenothiazines' describes the largest of the five main classes of neuroleptic antipsychotic drugs. These drugs have antipsychotic and, often, antiemetic properties, although they may also cause severe side effects such as extrapyramidal symptoms (including akathisia and tardive dyskinesia), hyperprolactinaemia, and the rare but potentially fatal neuroleptic malignant syndrome as well as substantial weight gain. |
Proton	The proton is a subatomic particle with the symbol p or p^+ and a positive electric charge of 1 elementary charge. One or more protons are present in the nucleus of each atom. The number of protons in each atom is its atomic number.
Proton pump	A proton pump is an integral membrane protein that is capable of moving protons across a biological membrane. Mechanisms are based on conformational changes of the protein structure or on the Q cycle.
Sulfonylurea	Sulfonylurea derivatives are a class of antidiabetic drugs that are used in the management of diabetes mellitus type 2. They act by increasing insulin release from the beta cells in the pancreas.
Thiazide	Thiazide is a type of molecule and a class of diuretics often used to treat hypertension and edema (such as that caused by heart, liver, or kidney disease).

The thiazides and thiazide-like diuretics reduce the risk of death, stroke, heart attack and heart failure due to hypertension. In most countries, the thiazides are the cheapest antihypertensive drugs available. |
Thyroid	The thyroid gland or simply, the thyroid, in vertebrate anatomy, is one of the largest endocrine glands. The thyroid gland is found in the neck, below the thyroid cartilage (which forms the laryngeal prominence, or 'Adam's apple'). The isthmus (the bridge between the two lobes of the thyroid) is located inferior to the cricoid cartilage.
Thyroid hormone	The thyroid hormones, triiodothyronine and thyroxine (T_4), are tyrosine-based hormones produced by the thyroid gland that are primarily responsible for regulation of metabolism. Iodine is necessary for the production of T_3 and T_4. A deficiency of iodine leads to decreased production of T_3 and T_4, enlarges the thyroid tissue and will cause the disease known as goitre.
Diuretic	A diuretic is any substance that promotes the production of urine. This includes forced diuresis. There are several categories of diuretics.

11. Pharmacology, Medication, and Intravenous Calculation Questions

Receptor antagonist	A receptor antagonist is a type of receptor ligand or drug that does not provoke a biological response itself upon binding to a receptor, but blocks or dampens agonist-mediated responses. In pharmacology, antagonists have affinity but no efficacy for their cognate receptors, and binding will disrupt the interaction and inhibit the function of an agonist or inverse agonist at receptors. Antagonists mediate their effects by binding to the active site or to allosteric sites on receptors, or they may interact at unique binding sites not normally involved in the biological regulation of the receptor's activity.
Intravenous	Intravenous therapy or IV therapy is the infusion of liquid substances directly into a vein. The word intravenous simply means 'within a vein'. Therapies administered intravenously are often called specialty pharmaceuticals.
Histamine	Histamine is an organic nitrogen compound involved in local immune responses as well as regulating physiological function in the gut and acting as a neurotransmitter. Histamine triggers the inflammatory response. As part of an immune response to foreign pathogens, histamine is produced by basophils and by mast cells found in nearby connective tissues.

1. Arginine vasopressin, also known as vasopressin, argipressin or _____ is a neurohypophysial hormone found in most mammals. Its two primary functions are to retain water in the body and to constrict blood vessels. Vasopressin regulates the body's retention of water by acting to increase water absorption in the collecting ducts of the kidney nephron.

   a. Aarhus University
   b. Antimycobacterial
   c. Antiparkinson
   d. Antidiuretic hormone

2. _____ is an examination for the licensing of nurses in the United States. There are two types, the _____-RN and the _____-PN.

   _____ examinations are developed and owned by the National Council of State Boards of Nursing, Inc. (NCSBN).

   a. Nightingale Pledge
   b. NCLEX
   c. Notes on Nursing
   d. Nurse Licensure Compact

3. _____ is a peptide hormone, produced by beta cells of the pancreas, and is central to regulating carbohydrate and fat metabolism in the body. _____ causes cells in the liver, skeletal muscles, and fat tissue to take up glucose from the blood. In the liver and skeletal muscles, glucose is stored as glycogen, and in adipocytes it is stored as triglycerides.

   a. Aarhus University
   b. Insulin
   c. Association for Computing Machinery
   d. Binding selectivity

4. _____s are a class of steroid hormones that are produced in the adrenal cortex. _____s are involved in a wide range of physiologic systems such as stress response, immune response and regulation of inflammation, carbohydrate metabolism, protein catabolism, blood electrolyte levels, and behavior. •Glucocorticoids such as cortisol control carbohydrate, fat and protein metabolism and are anti-inflammatory by preventing phospholipid release, decreasing eosinophil action and a number of other mechanisms.•Mineralocorticoids such as aldosterone control electrolyte and water levels, mainly by promoting sodium retention in the kidney.

   Some common natural hormones are corticosterone ($C_{21}H_{30}O_4$), cortisone ($C_{21}H_{28}O_5$, 17-hydroxy-11-dehydrocorticosterone) and aldosterone.

   a. Tissue fluid
   b. Dipeptidase
   c. Steapsin
   d. Corticosteroid

5. _____ (; MS Contin, MSIR, Avinza, Kadian, Oramorph, Roxanol, Kapanol) is a potent opiate analgesic drug that is used to relieve severe pain. It was first isolated in 1804 by Friedrich Sertürner, first distributed by him in 1817, and first commercially sold by Merck in 1827, which at the time was a single small chemists' shop. It was more widely used after the invention of the hypodermic needle in 1857. It took its name from the Greek god of dreams Morpheus .

   a. Naloxone
   b. Morphine
   c. Nitrofurantoin
   d. Nitrous oxide

1. d

2. b

3. b

4. d

5. b

You can take the complete Chapter Practice Test

for 11. Pharmacology, Medication, and Intravenous Calculation Questions
on all key terms, persons, places, and concepts.

Online 99 Cents

http://www.JustTheFacts101.com

Use www.JustTheFacts101.com for all your study needs

including Facts101's online interactive problem solving labs in

chemistry, statistics, mathematics, and more.

12. Additional Pyramid Strategies

_____	NCLEX
_____	Nursing school
_____	Pharmacology
_____	Toxic effects
_____	Renal function
_____	Carbonic anhydrase
_____	Fowler's position
_____	Sims' position

CHAPTER HIGHLIGHTS & NOTES: KEY TERMS, PEOPLE, PLACES, CONCEPTS

NCLEX	NCLEX is an examination for the licensing of nurses in the United States. There are two types, the NCLEX-RN and the NCLEX-PN. NCLEX examinations are developed and owned by the National Council of State Boards of Nursing, Inc. (NCSBN).
Nursing school	A nursing school is a type of educational institution, or part thereof, providing education and training to become a fully qualified nurse. The nature of nursing education and nursing qualifications varies considerably across the world.
Pharmacology	Pharmacology is the branch of medicine and biology concerned with the study of drug action, where a drug can be broadly defined as any man-made, natural, or endogenous (within the cell) molecule which exerts a biochemical and/or physiological effect on the cell, tissue, organ, or organism. More specifically, it is the study of the interactions that occur between a living organism and chemicals that affect normal or abnormal biochemical function. If substances have medicinal properties, they are considered pharmaceuticals.
Toxic effects	Toxicity is the degree to which a substance can damage an organism.

Toxicity can refer to the effect on a whole organism, such as an animal, bacterium, or plant, as well as the effect on a substructure of the organism, such as a cell (cytotoxicity) or an organ such as the liver (hepatotoxicity). By extension, the word may be metaphorically used to describe toxic effects on larger and more complex groups, such as the family unit or society at large.

Renal function

Renal function, in nephrology, is an indication of the state of the kidney and its role in renal physiology. Glomerular filtration rate (GFR) describes the flow rate of filtered fluid through the kidney. Creatinine clearance rate (C_{Cr} or CrCl) is the volume of blood plasma that is cleared of creatinine per unit time and is a useful measure for approximating the GFR. Creatinine clearance exceeds GFR due to creatinine secretion, which can be blocked by cimetidine.

Carbonic anhydrase

The carbonic anhydrases (or carbonate dehydratases) form a family of enzymes that catalyze the rapid interconversion of carbon dioxide and water to bicarbonate and protons (or vice-versa), a reversible reaction that occurs rather slowly in the absence of a catalyst. The active site of most carbonic anhydrases contains a zinc ion; they are therefore classified as metalloenzymes.

One of the functions of the enzyme in animals is to interconvert carbon dioxide and bicarbonate to maintain acid-base balance in blood and other tissues, and to help transport carbon dioxide out of tissues.

Fowler's position

In medicine, Fowler's position is a standard patient position. It is used to relax tension of the abdominal muscles, allowing for improved breathing in immobile patients as it alleviates compression of the chest due to gravity, and to increase comfort during eating and other activities. It is also used in postpartum women to improve uterine drainage.

Sims' position

The Sims' position is usually used for rectal examination, treatments and enemas. It is performed by having a patient lie on their left side, left hip and lower extremity straight, and right hip and knee bent. It is also called lateral recumbent position.

12. Additional Pyramid Strategies

1. The _____s (or carbonate dehydratases) form a family of enzymes that catalyze the rapid interconversion of carbon dioxide and water to bicarbonate and protons (or vice-versa), a reversible reaction that occurs rather slowly in the absence of a catalyst. The active site of most _____s contains a zinc ion; they are therefore classified as metalloenzymes.

    One of the functions of the enzyme in animals is to interconvert carbon dioxide and bicarbonate to maintain acid-base balance in blood and other tissues, and to help transport carbon dioxide out of tissues.

    a. Digestive enzyme
    b. Carbonic anhydrase
    c. Steapsin
    d. polymerase

2. _____ is the branch of medicine and biology concerned with the study of drug action, where a drug can be broadly defined as any man-made, natural, or endogenous (within the cell) molecule which exerts a biochemical and/or physiological effect on the cell, tissue, organ, or organism. More specifically, it is the study of the interactions that occur between a living organism and chemicals that affect normal or abnormal biochemical function. If substances have medicinal properties, they are considered pharmaceuticals.

    a. Bencao Gangmu
    b. Pharmacology
    c. Binding coefficient
    d. Binding selectivity

3. _____ is an examination for the licensing of nurses in the United States. There are two types, the _____-RN and the _____-PN.

    _____ examinations are developed and owned by the National Council of State Boards of Nursing, Inc. (NCSBN).

    a. Nightingale Pledge
    b. Nightingale ward
    c. NCLEX
    d. Nurse Licensure Compact

4. A _____ is a type of educational institution, or part thereof, providing education and training to become a fully qualified nurse. The nature of nursing education and nursing qualifications varies considerably across the world.

    a. Pinning ceremony
    b. Resusci Anne
    c. Nursing school
    d. Virtual patient

5. . Toxicity is the degree to which a substance can damage an organism.

Toxicity can refer to the effect on a whole organism, such as an animal, bacterium, or plant, as well as the effect on a substructure of the organism, such as a cell (cytotoxicity) or an organ such as the liver (hepatotoxicity). By extension, the word may be metaphorically used to describe _____ on larger and more complex groups, such as the family unit or society at large.

a. Tissue fluid
b. Benzodiazepine
c. Toxic effects
d. Binding selectivity

1. b
2. b
3. c
4. c
5. c

You can take the complete Chapter Practice Test

for 12. Additional Pyramid Strategies
on all key terms, persons, places, and concepts.

Online 99 Cents

http://www.JustTheFacts101.com

Use www.JustTheFacts101.com for all your study needs

including Facts101's online interactive problem solving labs in

chemistry, statistics, mathematics, and more.

13. Fundamental Skills Questions and Adult Health Questions

CHAPTER OUTLINE: KEY TERMS, PEOPLE, PLACES, CONCEPTS

	NCLEX
	Pharmacology
	Semi-vegetarian
	Nursing school

CHAPTER HIGHLIGHTS & NOTES: KEY TERMS, PEOPLE, PLACES, CONCEPTS

NCLEX	NCLEX is an examination for the licensing of nurses in the United States. There are two types, the NCLEX-RN and the NCLEX-PN. NCLEX examinations are developed and owned by the National Council of State Boards of Nursing, Inc. (NCSBN).
Pharmacology	Pharmacology is the branch of medicine and biology concerned with the study of drug action, where a drug can be broadly defined as any man-made, natural, or endogenous (within the cell) molecule which exerts a biochemical and/or physiological effect on the cell, tissue, organ, or organism. More specifically, it is the study of the interactions that occur between a living organism and chemicals that affect normal or abnormal biochemical function. If substances have medicinal properties, they are considered pharmaceuticals.
Semi-vegetarian	A semi-vegetarian or flexitarian diet is one that is plant-based with the occasional inclusion of meat products. In 2003, the American Dialect Society voted flexitarian as the year's most useful word and defined it as 'a vegetarian who occasionally eats meat'. In 2012, the term was listed for the first time in the mainstream Merriam-Webster's Collegiate Dictionary.
Nursing school	A nursing school is a type of educational institution, or part thereof, providing education and training to become a fully qualified nurse. The nature of nursing education and nursing qualifications varies considerably across the world.

13. Fundamental Skills Questions and Adult Health Questions

1. A _____ or flexitarian diet is one that is plant-based with the occasional inclusion of meat products. In 2003, the American Dialect Society voted flexitarian as the year's most useful word and defined it as 'a vegetarian who occasionally eats meat'. In 2012, the term was listed for the first time in the mainstream Merriam-Webster's Collegiate Dictionary.

   a. Flexitarian
   b. Tissue fluid
   c. Semi-vegetarian
   d. Binding selectivity

2. _____ is an examination for the licensing of nurses in the United States. There are two types, the _____-RN and the _____-PN.

   _____ examinations are developed and owned by the National Council of State Boards of Nursing, Inc. (NCSBN).

   a. NCLEX
   b. Nightingale ward
   c. Notes on Nursing
   d. Nurse Licensure Compact

3. _____ is the branch of medicine and biology concerned with the study of drug action, where a drug can be broadly defined as any man-made, natural, or endogenous (within the cell) molecule which exerts a biochemical and/or physiological effect on the cell, tissue, organ, or organism. More specifically, it is the study of the interactions that occur between a living organism and chemicals that affect normal or abnormal biochemical function. If substances have medicinal properties, they are considered pharmaceuticals.

   a. Bencao Gangmu
   b. Benzodiazepine
   c. Binding coefficient
   d. Pharmacology

4. A _____ is a type of educational institution, or part thereof, providing education and training to become a fully qualified nurse. The nature of nursing education and nursing qualifications varies considerably across the world.

   a. Nursing school
   b. Resusci Anne
   c. Simulated patient
   d. Virtual patient

1. c

2. a

3. d

4. a

You can take the complete Chapter Practice Test

for 13. Fundamental Skills Questions and Adult Health Questions
on all key terms, persons, places, and concepts.

Online 99 Cents

http://www.JustTheFacts101.com

Use www.JustTheFacts101.com for all your study needs

including Facts101's online interactive problem solving labs in

chemistry, statistics, mathematics, and more.

CPSIA information can be obtained at www.ICGtesting.com
Printed in the USA
LVOW09s2158121014

408455LV00001B/5/P